MW01235793

You Don't Intimidate Me

Overcoming the Spirit of Fear

Charles Roberts

Other great titles by Charles Roberts

101 Ways To Romance Your Wife God's Way

Every Man Is Not A Husband-Every Woman Is Not A

Wife

Take Authority

Faith Forward

*www.charlesrobertsonline.com **or** www.amazon.com*

Verses marked NIV are taken from the Holy Bible, New International Version®. Copyright © 1973, 1978, 1984 by the International Bible Society. Used by permission of Zondervan. All rights reserved. www.Zondervan.com

Unless otherwise indicated, all Scripture quotations are taken from the King James Version of the Bible. All rights reserved. No part of this book may be copied or reproduced in any form without written consent.

© 2012 by Charles Roberts

Edited by Carolyn Gregory

Please send all correspondence to printersway@yahoo.com or Charles Roberts, 2817 West End Ave Suite 126-217 Nashville, TN 37203 or visit *www.charlesrobertsonline.com* for more information.

Table of Contents

Introduction

All of us at some point in our lives have experienced fear. Many people spend years being gripped by the spirit of fear, never truly living the life Jesus died to provide for them. Even people of great faith have come face to face with this destructive weapon that Satan uses to paralyze God's people from moving forward. Some of the struggles people face are the fear of rejection, the fear of the unknown, the fear of other people, and the fear of failure to name a few. Turn on any television today and almost every program or newscast is fear based. It is challenging to find good positive programming that will encourage and inspire people to trust God by living a lifestyle of faith. Within a thirty-minute news broadcast, it is safe to say that the first twenty minutes transmits nothing but fear, where the reports are full of murders, robberies, and fatal accidents. Children are not immune to this crippling spirit, as they are exposed to fear by means of video games and movies that parents willingly purchase in an attempt to give them what they did not have while growing up. Throughout the Bible, God constantly instructed His people not to fear because He understands that living in fear is like trying to walk in quick sand. It immobilizes you so you cannot perform even the most basic task in life. Those who struggle with fear seem to have the deer-in-the-head-lights look, lacking the confidence it takes to step out and accomplish their God-given assignment.

The Word of God says, "We have not been given the spirit of fear, but of power, and of love, and of a sound mind" (2 Tim. 1:7). God has given us everything we need to overcome anything the enemy throws our way, and Satan knows this, which is why he fights so hard to keep God's people bound. Even as I am typing, fearful thoughts are bombarding my mind in an attempt to hinder me from equipping God's people with the truth that they have nothing to be afraid of because Christ has already overcome the world (John 16:33). Sadly, millions will spend their entire lives under the yoke and authority of Satan and his lies. Fear is defined as, a distressing emotion aroused by impending danger, evil, or pain, whether the threat is real or imagined. There is a great acronym for fear: False Evidence Appearing Real. Think about it, could it be the very thing you are afraid of does not even exist? That is what a lie is, something that does not exist. There is nothing that intimidates God, nothing. God's Word is more than enough to stand against those who oppose him. Knowing what Jesus did for us at Calvary, there should be nothing that intimidates a child of God. Genesis 1:26 says, "Let us make man, in our image, in our likeness." We have the same spiritual make-up as God. After Moses died, God told Joshua, "No one will be able to stand against you all the days of your life" (Joshua 1:5 NIV). Fear and every agent of fear is no match for a person once he or she knows who they are in Christ.

This book was written to empower God's people to take a stand against Satan and his lies. My desire is that every reader will go away with a holy boldness that enables them to face even the most disastrous circumstances. If you take the time and meditate on the Scriptures contained within, you too will have the same confession as David: "Though a host should encamp against me, my heart shall not fear" (Psalm 27:3). Allow the information contained within to take root and revolutionize your thinking so that when fear presents itself, you can confidently say, "*You Don't Intimidate Me!*"

The Enemy to Faith

I have heard it said that it is healthy to have a certain level of fear, but that is not what God says. Hebrews 11:6 says, "But without faith, it is impossible to please Him." Many fail to realize fear is an enemy to our most precious gift, the gift of faith, and will keep them from achieving what God says they can achieve through Him. According to the above-mentioned Scripture, God is displeased when we do not walk in faith. It grieves Him because He understands He is limited in moving in our lives, as He desire to. You see, God responds to faith. His ears are specifically tuned in to the faith frequency. God wants to do "exceeding, abundantly, above all you are able to ask or think of Him, according to the power that is at work within you" (Eph. 3:20). Notice He is going to do the impossible according to the power that is at work within you and not in Him, which is why it is important we guard the faith we receive from God's

Word. We as believers must be on the offensive when it comes to the things of God. We cannot provide Satan the opportunity to catch us off guard because if you give him an inch, he will take a yard. We cannot waiver as some do, but we must be "Steadfast, unmovable, always abounding in the work of the Lord" (1 Cor. 15:58). It is impossible to drive an automobile forward and in reverse at the same time, just as it is impossible to abide in faith and walk in fear at the same time. Fear is like a disease to your faith as it eats away at the core of your God-given potential.

Within each of us, God has deposited dreams, gifts, and talents that He wants to use to bless you and those around you. The problem is that if we allow our lives to be driven by fear, we will never be able to see the fullness of God's power operate in our lives. We have yet to see God move as He desires to. He wants to outdo Himself in and through our lives, but in order to do so we must give Him permission by abiding in faith. That's right. Our faith gives God permission to bless and heal us as His Word says. Actually, our faith is the platform God stands on when He wants to bless us.

Many fail to understand we have an adversary in Satan, and he wants to use fear to drive our lives off a cliff because his ultimate goal is to "steal, kill, and to destroy" (John 10:10). He will use any and everything at his disposal to move us out of faith and into fear. I am not suggesting that we will never feel afraid. What I am saying is even though fear may come, we must not give it permission to hinder or stop us in any way.

Believers are called to submit themselves unto God and God alone (Exodus 20:3). When we allow fear to be the driving force in our lives, in essence we are submitting to our fears with Satan being at the helm. No sane person would allow their enemy to baby-sit their children. This is because our children are vulnerable and precious gifts given to us by God. The same is true with our faith. Unless we take the initiative to feed our faith by spending time in the Word of God and in prayer, we are allowing the enemy to have full control over that which is most precious to us, our faith. The more time we spend meditating on God's Word, the stronger we will be so that when fear invades our lives, it is confronted and defeated with the truth.

If I were to walk into a dark room and immediately cut on the lights, darkness would become powerless, seeing as I have disarmed it with light. Let's say I had not eaten in two days. As soon as I consumed a meal, my hunger would no longer have power over me, having been destroyed by eating. This is what spending time in God's presence does for the believer. It arms us with that which we need to feed our faith and disarm every lie the enemy throws our way.

Our faith is one of the most valuable gifts God has given believers. We can lose everything we own, but by faith, we can regain that which was lost and even more. We can receive a bad report from our doctor with only a few days to live, but by faith, we can overcome the illness, living as much as 20 or 30 years longer. As long as we have faith, we have everything we will ever need to be the overcomer God says we are. The Word of God says, "This is the victory that has overcome the world, even our faith" (1 John 5:4 NIV). Faith is the victory!

Knowing that fear is the enemy to our faith, we should treat it as we would any other enemy in the natural. I know for myself if someone were to attempt to break into my home, I would do everything within my power to not only stop the intruder, but also deter the individual from any future attacks with an all-out assault on my part. The same should be true spiritually whenever Satan attempts to steal from God's people in any area of our lives. Jesus said, "The kingdom of heaven suffereth violence, and the violent take it by force" (Matt. 11:12). We must have an aggressive attitude if we are going to take something by force. It takes guts to be a Christian nowadays. I like to say it like this: We cannot be wimps and be Christians at the same time.

13

Let's say a couple has been standing in faith for ten years, hoping they will one day be the proud parents of their own little bundle of joy. Year after year, each attempt ends in another disappointment, and now they are beginning to lose hope they will ever be able to have a child. As the years pass and the wife grows older, fear begins to speak to her, telling her she is too old and that her time has come and gone. The couple has a choice. Do they listen to Satan's lies, allowing their fears to muffle their faith, or do they stand on God's Word, believing that "He is faithful that promised" (Heb. 10:23). Like this couple, we will have the opportunity to hold fast to the profession of our faith, or cave in under the pressure that fear will most assuredly apply.

As mentioned previously, I am not suggesting because a person may live a lifestyle of faith that fear will never be an issue. God is calling His children to stand strong in the midst of fear. True strength is when we can press forward even in the midst of difficult circumstances. Fear may be screaming on the inside, saying we're never going to make it, but true overcomers keep going, relying on their faith in God to see them through.

The Bible is full of examples of great men and women who never gave up in spite of the challenges they faced. Moses instructed the children of Israel to "Be strong and of a good courage, fear not, nor be afraid" (Deut. 31:6). After Moses' death, God instructed Joshua three times to "Be strong and of a good courage" (Josh. 1:6-9). Finally, before his death, King David instructed Solomon to "Be strong, and act like a man" (1 Kings 2:2 NIV).

It takes faith to keep going forward, even when there are no visible signs in the natural that anything is changing. It takes faith to continually give, even when our bank account may be running in the red. It takes faith to trust that God will come through, even though everything that could go wrong does.

In order to live the victorious life God has called us to live, we must defeat the enemy of fear by consistently applying the Word of God when challenges arise. Then and only then will we be able to walk in the level of faith God intended.

Personal Points

Those who know me would be surprised to learn that growing up I struggled with the spirit of fear. The enemy would attack me, and since I was not spirit-filled, I did not realize nor understand what was going on. I had very low self-esteem, so much so that I hated myself. I also struggled with people pleasing, attempting to keep everyone around me happy. Living a life where I attempted to keep everyone happy was tiresome, and I suffered severely. Because I had a tainted view of God and myself, it was difficult for me to receive God's love. I just could not grasp the idea that God would extend unconditional love to me, and no matter how many times people encouraged me, it never registered. This is how the spirit of fear operates. It is relentless with its lies, and unless you take the initiative to change your thinking, it will pull you down into the abyss of hopelessness and despair. It was only until I reprogrammed my mind with God's

Word that I was able to break free. This was not an easy task; neither did I change overnight. In fact, this is something I still do every day of my life, but the good news is I now know who I am in Christ.

The Voice of Fear

For those who are parents, it is safe to say their ears are well tuned to the sounds of their children, even though there may be many other sounds that are louder. This is because parents are familiar with the voice of their child. Fear has a voice, and it is imperative that believers become familiar with it so that it does not rob us of the life God has ordained for us. When speaking about His followers, Jesus said, "But they will never follow a stranger; in fact, they will run away from him because they do not recognize a stranger's voice" (John 10:5 NIV). Followers of Jesus should consider the voice of fear to be a stranger that attempts to steer them from the will of God. Sadly, many have been deceived, thinking they are following God when actually they are following the voice of fear. Only by consistently reading and meditating on God's Word will we be able to discern the voice of fear when it speaks. The Bible says, "Faith cometh by hearing, and hearing by the word of God" (Rom. 10:17). Notice that our ability to hear is linked to God's Word. This means the less Word we have; the less likely we are able to hear, meaning we could be led by any voice that speaks.

Believers need to understand that the voice of fear can speak internally or externally, either through the life of another person or the individual themselves. How many times have you believed you heard from the Lord to act on something, only to have your mind bombarded with fearful thoughts, causing you to abandon God's instruction? This is a perfect example of the voice of fear speaking internally. A biblical example of fear speaking externally can be seen in the gospel of Matthew where Peter pulled Jesus aside after He told His disciples He would suffer many things and be killed. Peter said; "Be it far from thee Lord: this shall not be unto thee" (Matt. 16:22). That was not faith speaking but fear, and Jesus recognized it as such and immediately dealt with it accordingly. Many Christians fail to recognize the voice of fear because quite often it speaks through a vessel we are most familiar with. It is important for us to remember that anyone whose mind has not been renewed by the Word of God can be used by Satan to inject fear in our lives. This was the case with Peter, and we are no different. Maybe you have always dreamed of traveling the world, or stepping out and launching your own business, and without thinking, you shared your dream with others. What you must understand is not everyone will appreciate the dream that God has given you, and whether done intentionally or not, others may say things that will cause you to abort what God says you can accomplish. This was the case with Joseph, when he shared his dream with his brothers. The Scripture says, "Joseph had a dream, and when he told it to his brothers, they hated him all the more" (Gen. 37:5 NIV). Because there is such a great call on your life, you must realize that sometimes your dream can cause resentment and even hatred in others, which gets its roots from fear. Fear says, "I'm too afraid to step out and do something myself, and because of this I don't want you to do anything either."

If we are going to be successful in overcoming the spirit of fear, not only will we have to discern the voice of fear, but we must also identify those who Satan uses to speak fear into our lives. Just because a person attends church every week does not mean they are spiritually mature enough to handle the call of God on your life. We must focus if we are going to give birth to what God has placed within us. Consider a racehorse, how it wears blinders so it cannot see the other horses on either side. By wearing blinders, it allows the horse to focus its attention straight ahead and not on the other horses on the left or the right. The same is true in the life of a believer. In order to overcome the spirit of fear, we must wear spiritual blinders by not giving attention to people or things that seek to pull us out of faith. Proverbs 4:23 says, "Keep thy heart with all diligence; for out of it are the issues of life." To keep your heart means we must pay close attention to what we listen to, what we look at, what we say, and what we think. All of these are entry points leading to our hearts, but if we do not know this, then it will be very easy for Satan to have his way in our lives.

As of late, stock markets around the world have been driven by fear. Investors hear rumors that one nation may go bankrupt, so they begin pulling their money out, fearing they will lose if they hold their current positions. On the other hand, they hear a report that says it is best to invest in commodities, as they are a safer bet than financial stocks. Notice they made their decisions based on fear. We must never allow ourselves to be led by the spirit of fear because in the end, we will always regret our decision.

There will be times when we are surrounded by individuals who are led by the spirit of fear, or at the very least are speaking doubt and unbelief, and we are unable to avoid them. We will not be able to separate ourselves from everyone, which is why it is critical that we build ourselves up through prayer so we will be able to withstand the attacks that are sure to come. As we grow stronger in the Lord, He will enable us to stand firm in the midst of dire circumstances, while everyone else is worried and anxious.

When God created the world, He did it through the spoken Word. Each time He got ready to create something, the Bible says, "And God said" (Gen. 1:3). God spoke faith, and creation came to be. Consequently, the enemy speaks fear, but instead of creating something, it brings about destruction. Our words are very powerful because we are made in the image and likeness of God. This is why it is crucial we do not give the voice of fear access to our mouths, so that it will not be able to bring destruction in our lives.

The beauty of the resurrection is that Jesus duplicated Himself and although He is now in heaven, His spirit lives within humanity. When we accept Christ as our Lord and Savior, the Spirit of God quickens us, enabling us to live the life God intended. If we never accept Jesus, or if we accept Him but never adhere to His Word, we are susceptible to being filled with the spirit of fear, which we have already established seeks to "steal, kill, and to destroy" (John 10:10). Just as God desired to duplicate Himself, so does the enemy, and the way he does it is by keeping us ignorant to what has already been provided for us by way of the cross. When we know who we are in Christ, we understand that our words have creative power and we will be mindful about what we say. When we know who we are in Christ, we will not be moved whenever we hear bad news, because we know God is in control. Finally, when we know who we are in Christ, we can distinguish between the voice of fear over every other voice that is speaking, and cast down the lies Satan hurls our way.

Personal Points

I grew up in the Catholic Church, and as an adult, I decided to find a church that would fill my spiritual hunger. I opted for a nondenominational church, or Word of Faith church as it is called. I loved it. I learned more in one Sunday than I did my entire life at the Catholic Church. I will never forget the battle I fought over my thoughts. I noticed the more of God's Word I received, the harder I struggled with my thoughts, so much so that I had blasphemous thoughts race through my mind. I literally thought I was going crazy. I lost weight, and my hair was quickly turning gray. One day while at work I noticed my hand was shaking uncontrollably. I remember asking the Lord what was going on with me and He told me that I was no different than a former drug addict who was being weaned off drugs. Since I was receiving God's Word, Satan hated it and was doing everything in his power to draw me back into darkness. I truly believe the moment we receive Christ is the most critical time in our lives because we are vulnerable to go backward unless we are in an environment of love where God's Word is taught.

The Characteristics of Fear

During flu season millions of people seek treatment from their doctors in an attempt to relieve symptoms such as a runny nose, congestion, and a high temperature. By describing their symptoms in detail to their physician, it makes it easier for the physician to correctly diagnose and treat patients. Just as an individual with the flu has symptoms, the same is true with an individual who is gripped by the spirit of fear. Fear is crippling, and not only does it cause great emotional stress but physical stress as well such as sleeplessness, anxiousness, fatigue, upset stomach, racing thoughts, and isolation. Just writing these makes me feel uneasy. None of these represents what Jesus came to provide for us when He died on the cross. Jesus said, "I am come that they might have life, and that they might have it more abundantly" (John 10:10). I do not know about you, but when I think about some of the symptoms or characteristics of fear, they do not sound very abundant to me. On the contrary, they sound like they seek to steal from an individual instead of adding to a person's life.

In looking at the life of Job, we see how he was led by the spirit of fear and gave strength to his fears through his words and actions. In Job 1, God established that Job was a perfect and upright man who feared or reverenced God. Job had everything a person could desire. He had seven sons and three daughters. He possessed thousands of animals, which during that time was a symbol of great wealth. His family was close knit as they would often come together to celebrate various feast days. We see the first sign of fear in Job 1:5 where it says, "When a period of feasting had run its course, Job would make arrangements for them to be purified. Early in the morning, he would sacrifice a burnt offering for each of them, thinking; perhaps my children have sinned and cursed God in their hearts. This was Job's regular custom" (Job 1:5 NIV). The first significant point is that Job automatically thought negatively about his children, fearing they may have sinned against God. The Bible never says any of his children sinned, but Job felt it necessary to offer a sacrifice just in case. This is how fear operates. It assumes the worse and then takes steps to provide a solution, even though there is no visible proof that anything occurred. Job was feeding his fears with his actions. Whenever we give strength to our fears by acting on them, we set ourselves up to receive what we feared, as was the case with Job. We later see Job suffered great losses: His children were killed and his possessions were destroyed and looted. Job 3:25 says, "For the thing which I greatly feared is come upon me, and that which I was afraid of is come unto me." Job should have guarded his heart, choosing his thoughts carefully so fear would not have the chance to take root. Because he did not, this gave birth to actions that were not led by faith but fear. Our thoughts play a major role in overcoming the spirit of fear, which is why we are commanded to "cast down imaginations, and every high thing that exalts itself against the knowledge of God, bringing into captivity every thought to the obedience of Christ" (2 Cor. 10:5). Wrong thoughts lead to wrong words, and wrong words lead to wrong actions.

Another characteristic of fear is isolation when we become embarrassed when a sin is committed. We serve a loving and forgiving God, but sadly, many of us fail to receive His forgiveness when we fall short. Far too many Christians have left the church out of embarrassment because of something they have done, thinking God or people could never forgive them. This is far from the truth. Sure there are some people who will always hold things against us when we fall short, but they are not God. The only opinion that matters is God's, and He says we are forgiven. Consider the example of Adam and Eve. "And they heard the voice of the Lord God walking in the garden in the cool of the day: and Adam and his wife hid themselves from the presence of the Lord God amongst the trees of the garden" (Gen. 3:8). Notice that Adam and Eve sought to isolate themselves from the presence of God due to their disobedience. How many times

31

have you done or said something wrong and maybe for a brief period, sought the comfort of being alone? Well, Jesus' sacrifice made it possible for every person to wipe the slate clean, which means the only thing keeping a person from receiving God's forgiveness is fear. Fear will lie to us, causing us to believe what we did was too over the top and that God could never accept us back. The spirit of fear likes to deal in absolutes, but not our God. He is not the God of a second chance; He is the God of another chance. Satan knows if he can get us to isolate ourselves, he has a greater chance of bringing about the destruction in our lives he desires.

I believe millions of people struggle with the spirit of fear, and they do not even realize it. We only need to look at the state of the world, with the rapid advancement of immorality, and it is proof that fear has gripped the hearts and minds of God's people. There is a famous quote by Edmund Burke that says, "The only thing necessary for the triumph of evil is for good men to do nothing" (Bartlett's

Familiar Quotations, 15th ed.). If more of us who profess Christ would stand up against those who work in opposition to God, our world would be much different. Sadly, many of us feel like it's someone else's job to do the difficult task of fighting against the kingdom of darkness. We would rather stand on the sidelines and complain, offering criticism toward pastors, community leaders, and anyone who dares to take a step of faith and engage themselves in battle. Those who do make the courageous choice to take God at His Word often fight the hardest against those who claim to be on their side, and the main reason is fear. Fearful people are intimidated by change of any kind. We cannot be true believers and not be willing to change. Change is a part of the Christian walk. A person can sit in a garage all day, yet that will not make him a car, just as someone could be in church for twenty or thirty years but that does not mean he is a faith-filled believer. Faith is always in motion, always progressing toward the promises of God. Fear is the total opposite - nothing more than faith in reverse and is a sin. Fear says that one does not believe that God is able to do anything. God can do more in the life of one person who takes Him at His Word than billions who waiver, doubting He can or will come through for them. The Bible instructs us that when we approach God, we are to ask in faith and not doubt, because the one who doubts is like a wave of the sea, blown and tossed by the wind (James 1:6). Billions of blessings have gone unclaimed because we have allowed the spirit of fear to be the driving force in our lives, and not God's Word.

The spirit of fear is a deadly weapon we must stand in faith against, or it will rob us of everything that pertains to life. Our health, finances, family, dreams, and aspirations are all targeted by fear, making it crucial to spend quality time building ourselves up spiritually. In the next chapter, we will discuss the proper response to the spirit of fear and provide biblical examples of those that overcame the most dire circumstances.

Personal Points

I listened to Satan's lies for years, so much so that my stomach would burn from stress and anxiousness, which are characteristics of fear. I believe many Christians suffer just as I did but are afraid to admit it. The sad thing about it was I was in church the whole time, acting as if nothing were wrong but living a lie. As I grew in my knowledge of God, I learned how to relax and just settle down. Living a life of faith is liberating. I would go so far as to say that a person has not really lived until they live a lifestyle of faith.

The Response to Fear

I have come to understand that the best way to handle a bully is not give in to his demands, but call his bluff, attacking him with an all-out assault if necessary. The same approach should be taken when it comes to dealing with the spirit of fear. This demonic spirit is nothing more than a bully, seeking to push God's people around until we willingly hand over everything God has given us. Today I have great news for all of God's children: We don't have to put up with the bully of fear another day. All we need to do is call the Devil's bluff and attack. Take a stand, draw a line in the sand, and put all of hell on notice, declaring, "Satan, you were defeated on Calvary, and now I'm here to enforce your defeat. Take your hands off my family. Take your hands off my finances. Take your hands off my possessions." Just imagine yourself grabbing that stupid Devil by the throat, picking him up off the ground, and staring him in the face, letting him know you're not putting up with his foolishness another day! Some may say this is farfetched, but this is the authority Jesus has given every born-again believer. The problem is most Christians do not fully understand the power we possess and we allow ourselves to be intimidated by an adversary that has already been defeated. The size of your giant should not determine your response. The response to fear should always be the same, that being, *"You Don't Intimidate Me!"*

Let's examine the life of David and how he responded when he faced the giant, Goliath. The Philistine army had gathered to do battle against the children of Israel at a place called Shochoh and Azekah (1 Sam. 17:1). Verse 4 says, "A champion named Goliath, who was from Gath, came out of the Philistine camp. His height was six cubits and a span. He had a bronze helmet on his head and wore a coat of scale armor of bronze weighing five thousand shekels" (1 Sam. 17:4-5 NIV). The Israelite army was obviously afraid when they laid eyes on Goliath and were defeated before a single arrow was shot. This is why it is important that we guard our hearts, not allowing what our natural eyes see to keep us from advancing forward. The enemy has won far too many battles before they even began because we have given up after looking at the size of the enemy. This was true for everyone that day, everyone except for David. When David heard the voice of the enemy insult God's people, he asked, "Who is this uncircumcised Philistine, that he should defy the armies of the living God" (1 Sam. 17:26 NIV)? I would argue the battle was over at the point when David asked this question, for no matter how big Goliath was, or how small David was, his faith in God was big enough to overcome any obstacle. When Goliath saw David, he mocked him, saying, "Am I a dog, that you come at me with sticks? And the Philistine cursed David by his gods" (1 Sam. 17:43 NIV). When our enemy looks at us, he laughs because of our weapons of choice. Never underestimate that which God has placed in your hand to defeat your adversary. Perhaps your dream is to operate your own photography studio but all you have is a camera. The spirit of fear will tell you that you do not have enough, but with God, that is all you need. Someone else may have a dream to further their education so they might be more marketable to prospective employers, but all they have is an old laptop. The spirit of fear will tell you that you will never be able to get ahead, and you might as well give up now. Let me boldly say you can do more with less as long as you have God's anointing, which is what David had. Instead of shrinking back in fear, David announced to Goliath, "You come against me with sword and spear and javelin, but I come against you in the name of the Lord Almighty, the God of the armies of Israel, whom you have defied. This day the Lord will deliver you into my hands, and I'll strike you down and cut off your head. This very day I will give the carcasses of the Philistine army to the birds and the wild animals, and the whole world will know that there is a God in Israel" (1 Sam. 17:45-46 NIV). Wow, now that is how one should respond to the spirit of fear! Notice David never considered the size of his stature nor his weaponry. He just made the bold proclamation that God would give him the victory over the enemy.

God expects all of His children to respond in faith just as David did. Whenever we allow ourselves to be intimidated by the enemy, it is an affront to God because His Word says that we are more than conquerors (Rom. 8:37). Nothing is impossible to them that believe that God can do anything (Mark 9:23). What has the spirit of fear told you that you will never be able to accomplish? What lies have you been listening to repeatedly? Whatever the spirit of fear has told you, recognize it as a lie. You can do anything God's Word says. Since we know that Satan is a liar and the father of it, why waste valuable time listening to him? Me personally, I do not like to waste my time, especially when it involves listening to someone who does not tell the truth. Sure Satan will run his mouth, but God has given us authority over him and we should respond accordingly. Stop being afraid of someone who was conquered in front of the whole world. Gird yourself up and stand your ground, and let the forces of darkness know they have a fight on their hands if they even attempt to mess with you. Take the fight to the Devil and attack him with your prayers, your praise, and your actions. David did. He did not wait; he took the fight to his enemy, which is what God is waiting on us to do. The Bible says, "And it came to pass, when the Philistine arose, and came and drew nigh to meet David, that David hasted, and ran toward the army to meet the Philistine (1 Sam. 17:48). We must stop allowing the spirit of fear to run all over us. Ok, so you have more month than money. That does not mean you should just curl up in a corner and allow the Devil to destroy you physically, emotionally, and financially. Know that "greater is He that is within you than he that is in the world" (1 John 4:4).

When we receive Jesus as Lord and Savior, He comes to reside within us and promises to never leave us nor forsake us (Heb. 13:5). Since God's Spirit dwells within us, there is nothing we will ever face that can overpower us unless we allow it. We are the only ones who can give the enemy permission to destroy our lives. Having our faith anchored in God will cancel every scheme and strategy the spirit of fear will try to use against us.

Laugh at the spirit of fear

Whenever we feel the spirit of fear coming against us, our first response should be to laugh. That's right, I said laugh. This is what God does. The Bible says, "The One enthroned in heaven laughs; the Lord scoffs at them" (Psalm 2:4 NIV). The Lord laughs because He knows Satan is already defeated, and He is waiting on us to laugh with Him. It confuses Satan when we laugh at him instead of cringing in fear, when our response does not match our circumstances. In the natural, we should have given up a long time ago, and the enemy cannot understand why we keep believing, which demoralizes him. I can see Satan now asking the question, "Don't they know they're bankrupt? Don't they know they have been sick for years? Don't they know they are defeated?" Our response should be, No I don't know! A person who refuses to give up is like a thorn in Satan's side. Satan knows he has tried everything in his arsenal but the believer refuses to quit. We may be bruised, battered, and tired, but as long as we continue to press forward, it is sure to bring Satan to his knees.

If we are going to have any success against the enemy, we must possess aggressive faith, which does not seat idly by allowing Satan to have his way, but prepares itsclf for the battle that awaits us. The Bible says that our adversary, "Walketh about, seeking whom he may devour" (1 Peter 5:8). Notice how the enemy operates. He prowls like a lion. The word *prowl* means to move stealthily, seeking prey. Since we already know Satan is seeking us stealthily, why not be bold and go on the offensive, taking the fight to him? I would go so far to suggest that God encourages believers to walk in this level of faith, with a great example being the children of Israel in the Book of Joshua. When speaking to Joshua, God said, "And ye shall compass the city, all ye men of war, and go round about the city once. Thus shalt thou do six days" (Josh. 6:3). Notice this type of faith was not passive, just waiting on the enemy to attack, but aggressive, letting the enemy know, "here we are, get ready." No one goes into battle thinking he is going to lose. He goes into battle with the expectation that not only will he win, but that he already has the victory.

Our response to the spirit of fear should always be, "I hear you running your mouth, and I'm not afraid of you anymore. You may have dictated my actions in the past, but those days are over. From now on I'm calling the shots and according to the Word of God, I win!" Be bold and confident in who God says you are, knowing that all of heaven is on your side. Take your life back today by responding to the spirit of fear with the faith of God, knowing you cannot lose because you have already won.

Personal Points

The man I am today and the person I use to be are like night and day. Instead of cringing in fear, I now welcome the challenge of engaging Satan in spiritual battle. I even asked the Lord what was wrong with me because I actually get excited with the struggle. I think this has something to do with my competitive nature because I hate to lose more than I like to win. I now view Satan as an opponent who is standing in my way, and just like every opponent from my past, he must be defeated. The good news for me is because of what Jesus did on Calvary, Satan has already been defeated, and all I have to do is enforce his defeat.

Floor It

Have you ever been trying to get somewhere in a hurry and somehow you ended up behind a timid driver who constantly accelerates and then brakes repeatedly? It is as if they cannot make up their minds what they want to do, all while your heart is racing because you know if you cannot get ahead of them soon, you will be late. After a few miles, you see an opening and without hesitation, you floor it, not only passing them, but leaving them in the dust. This is what we should do if we are going to overcome the spirit of fear: We should floor it. This means we must take the necessary steps to leave behind every wrong mind-set, every negative person, and every fear if we are going to fulfill the destiny God has for our lives. There are people yet to be born whose futures are depending on us overcoming our fears and fulfilling our dreams. The enemy wants to keep us stuck in a rut, replaying the same lies in our minds, but we must take those thoughts captive and cast down every imagination, and high thing that exalts itself against the knowledge of God (2 Cor. 10:5). This cannot be done casually; we must floor it past dead-end thinking. If we have people in our lives who tend to pull down our spirit with their gloom and doom speech, we must floor it out of that relationship, or it will poison our futures.

We cannot play around with fear, or it will leave us trapped without our knowledge. One of the best ways to leave fear in the dust is by arming ourselves with the truth. When we know the truth, then it is easy to detect a lie when it presents itself. Jesus said, "I am the way, I am the truth and the life" (John 14:6). The truth is liberating and a place of rest, regardless of what is going on in the natural. In the natural, the spirit of fear may say, "The economy has been down a long time, you will never be able to find a job." The truth of God's Word says, "But my God shall supply all your need according to His riches in glory by Christ Jesus" (Phil. 4:19). The spirit of fear may say, "You are getting up in age; you will never have a child," but God's Word says, "All the promises of God in him are yea and in Him amen" (2 Cor. 1:20). When Satan starts running his mouth, you should immediately start running yours, flooring past his lies with the truth. Do not allow his lies to take root in your heart, but respond swiftly and in the authority that Jesus provided.

Many fail to realize the true power that resides in faith. Faith can take us where money cannot. Faith can open doors that education could never open. That is how powerful faith is, and unless we take steps to consistently and aggressively feed our faith and starve our doubts, then this gives fear permission to move in and plunder every area of our lives.

Have you ever been home relaxing when all of a sudden an unwanted houseguest shows up and stays longer than you would have liked? Not only did he come at an inconvenient time, but he took it upon himself to peruse through your home without permission. Consider the spirit of fear the same as an unwanted houseguest. It shows up uninvited, seeking to invade every area of your life until it takes over, leaving you mentally, physically, financially, and spiritually bankrupt. This is why it is so important to keep one's foot on the gas and floored past fear and in faith. The good news for us is that it does not take much faith to accomplish great things for God. Jesus said, "If you have faith as a grain of mustard seed, ye shall say unto this mountain, remove hence to yonder place; and it shall remove; and nothing shall be impossible unto you" (Matt. 17:20). There is nothing that a born-again believer cannot accomplish in this life as long as they abide in faith. Your faith will never fail you because God never fails. As long as you remain steadfast on what God says, nothing shall be impossible for you.

There are places God wants to take us and things He wants to do in and through our lives, we cannot imagine, and Satan knows it. Christians are his number one target, and he will do any and everything he can to destroy us. Think of it this way. What would be your response if I walked up to you and told you, "I hate everything about you and what you stand for, and if given the opportunity, I'm going to take you out?" How would you react every time you saw me? Well, Satan has already come out and stated he hates our guts and wants to wipe us off the face of the planet, with one of his methods being the spirit of fear. Sadly, millions of Christians know Satan's intentions, but fail to take the necessary steps to guard themselves. It was God who said, "My people are destroyed for lack of knowledge" (Hos. 4:6). We cannot become so complacent where we do not recognize the impending dangers that await us. Many sit back waiting, expecting God to fight their battles for them. Please understand, the last thing Jesus said on the cross was, "It is finished" (John 19:30). This means He has done all He is going to do and has given us the authority to enforce Satan's defeat. Not only is God waiting on us, but all of creation is waiting on us to take our rightful place and walk in our spiritual authority. The Bible says, "For the creation waits in eager expectation for the children of God to be revealed" (Rom. 8:19 NIV).

Your life is not just about you. You cannot just sit back, wasting precious time, allowing the enemy to divert the plan of God for your life. Get up and engage Satan on the battlefield. Floor it into your destiny, your future is waiting.

Personal Points

When I was younger in my faith, I was told by a great man of God that in order to be a successful Christian, I must spend quality time reading my Bible. He went on to say that I must seek God in prayer and seek Him early. I struggled with this at first. There were times when I would wake up an hour early, only to fall asleep, sometimes on my knees. As I continued to press through, I no longer have a problem getting up early to spend time with the Lord. Now I love reading my Bible, especially Proverbs because it is so rich with wisdom. I have learned that the more of God's Word I apply to my life, the stronger I am against Satan's attacks. My faith has grown leaps and bounds to where it was before, and I cannot wait to see where God will take me in the years to come.

Know Your Enemy

In order to overcome every strategy Satan will use, we must understand why he does what he does. What is important to remember is that Satan is a copycat who wants to be just like God. All we have to do is look at Scripture and we will see what caused Satan's downfall, as well as his method of operation, so that we can be victorious against him every time. The first point worth noting is that Satan was kicked out of heaven because of pride. "How you have fallen from heaven, morning star, son of the dawn! You have been cast down to the earth, you who once laid low the nations! You said in your heart, I will ascend to the heavens; I will raise my throne above the stars of God; I will sit enthroned on the mount of assembly, on the utmost heights of Mount Zaphon. I will ascend above the tops of the clouds; I will make myself like the Most High" (Isaiah 14:12-14 NIV). Satan is full of pride because no one in his right mind would ever attempt to go against God and think he will win. Because Satan is full of pride, his strategy against us will be bold and aggressive, and he will fight dirty in an effort to win. One of the reasons he uses fear against people is for control. If I can get you to be afraid, then I can control you and get you to do what I want.

Fear keeps us bound so that we have limited movement. For example, when I was a child, my cousins and I would walk home from school every day. They were older than I was and on one particular day, they told me that if I stepped on a mushroom then I would turn into one. For years, I avoided mushrooms whenever I walked. If I saw one, I would make sure to give myself enough room so that my foot never came near it. I was being controlled by fear, and it was only after I got a revelation of the truth did I feel comfortable around mushrooms. Although this is a humorous exaggeration, sadly, millions of Christians are being controlled by fear and do not even realize it. Satan uses fear to keep Christians from witnessing to others about the Lord. He uses fear to keep people from coming to church, and he also uses fear to keep people from standing up for what is right.

The spirit of fear is no match for a person when he knows who he is in Christ. On one occasion, Jesus was praying to the Father about eternal life, and He said, "And this is life eternal, that they might know thee the only true God, and Jesus Christ, whom thou hast sent" (John 17:3). In order to overcome the spirit of fear, we must have a revelation of who God is because once we do, He will give us a revelation of who we are in Him. This is why close fellowship with the Father is crucial because it reveals things, giving understanding to our hearts we could not have otherwise.

I hate it when I see people living well below their God-given potential, especially when the only thing holding them back is fear. Millions of Christians have been praying for financial breakthrough for years but are allowing fear to keep them from tithing, thinking they will not have enough left over. Some are struggling, working the same dead-end job, but are too afraid to take a chance and start a business because they heard how others did so and failed. This is Satan's goal. He does not want us to trust God. If we do, Satan will lose his control. We were created to rule the earth and have dominion, not to be ruled and dominated. Most are afraid of an enemy whom they have authority over. This may sound crazy but it has been happening for years and will continue to happen until we come to the full knowledge of the truth.

Another reason Satan uses fear as a method of control is because he wants people to worship him instead of God. We have already established that he was kicked out of heaven because he wanted to be like God, and one of the ways he attempts to copy God is by getting people to worship him. A great example of this can be seen in the Book of Matthew where it says, "Again the devil taketh him up into an exceeding high mountain, and sheweth him all the kingdoms of the world, and the glory of them. And saith unto him, All these things will I

You Don't Intimidate Me

give thee, if thou wilt fall down and worship me" (Matt. 4:8-9). Nothing about Satan is original, and because he has a warped mind, he was foolish enough to tempt Jesus to worship him. Sadly, millions of people have fallen for this same trick and still do, with many being Christians. We might say, "I would never worship Satan" and yet do it every day when we put worldly affections above God. We worship Satan when we miss church so we can attend a sporting event. We worship Satan when we take the money that God gives us through our jobs and use it for personal reasons. All of these may sound over the top, but not according to God. He expects our total allegiance to Him. I would go so far as to say that everything in life is about worship. We are either worshipping God or worshipping the Devil.

One of the attributes of fear is selfishness. Selfishness and fear go hand in hand because people who struggle with fear have their minds on themselves and not on God's Word. Scripture says, "Thou will keep them in perfect peace whose mind is stayed on thee: because he trusteth in thee" (Isa. 26:3). We are guaranteed to be kept in a state of perpetual peace when we have our very being fixated on God's Word. It is only when we take our eyes off God that fear creeps in and tells us all the things we cannot accomplish. The enemy loves to keep us consumed with ourselves-what is not going right in our lives, how people hurt us, and how nothing good ever happens to us. These are all lies spoken from the mouth of Satan and should be recognized as such. I am not suggesting when unfair things happen that they should be minimized. What I am saying is we cannot allow fear and how we feel affect our obedience to God. Whenever we get to the point where our thoughts and words are all about us, that is a good time to stop and ask the lord to help, then casting our cares upon Him, because He cares for us (1 Pet. 5:7).

God has already walked every step of your life, and He is waiting at the end with hopes that you will accomplish everything He said you could accomplish through Him. The spirit of fear will be at every turn, attempting to delay, derail, and thwart the plan of God, and it is up to you whether you will allow it to happen. You and God are an unstoppable force, so regardless of the tactics Satan will use against you, you are destined to prevail as you keep God's Word before you.

Personal Points

My great-grandmother, whom we affectionately called Mama Neal, used to always tell me, "Baby, don't ever let people know how much sense you have." This was some of the best advice she ever gave me, and it means do not go through life showing all your cards. This is what I do with Satan. In knowing your enemy, it is important not to reveal everything to him or you set yourself up to be attacked. I make a habit of never sharing a personal problem with someone who is not qualified nor has the means to solve the problem. Neither do I share my dreams with just anyone. The dreams God gives us are precious and if shared with the wrong people, can create an environment of jealousy and resentment. Examine Joseph's life and you will understand what I mean (Gen. 37:5-11).

Bully the Bully

If there is one thing I cannot stand, it is a bully. Bullies are the lowest of the low. They tend to pick on people for no apparent reason other than for enjoyment. A bully usually picks on those he thinks he can intimidate. I have never seen a bully pick a fight with someone that is bigger than he is. This being the case, I do not understand why so many Christians allow the Devil to intimidate them with the spirit of fear, seeing as we are greater and possess a power that has no equal. We have the Spirit of God within us, and the Devil and all of hell is no match for us. One born-again, blood-washed believer has more power than all the demons of hell combined. Instead of Satan having the audacity to try to bully us around, we as believers should be so bold as to seek to bully the Devil. We can do this by flooding the hospitals and healing the sick. Providing for the homeless and teaching them about the love of Jesus. Taking authority over drug-infested neighborhoods, and ridding them of those

You Don't Intimidate Me

that seek to destroy the lives of others. Holding unrighteous government officials accountable, informing them they will no longer be allowed to pass laws contrary to the Word of God. Finally, we can inform Hollywood that profanity and nudity is no longer acceptable, and if they want to make a profit, they had better start producing quality material.

We have been given authority over Satan, not the other way around. It matters not if we are outnumbered; what matters is that we have the advantage because we have the Spirit of the Lord. There is a great story of how the Spirit of God came upon Samson and enabled him to kill one thousand men. Scripture says, "As he approached Lehi, the Philistines came toward him shouting. The Spirit of the Lord came powerfully upon him. The ropes on his arms became like charred flax, and the bindings dropped from his hands. Finding a fresh jawbone of a donkey, he grabbed it and struck down a thousand men" (Jud. 15:14-15 NIV). Notice Samson was not intimidated by the number of those who were against him; he was confident his God was greater than any enemy he would face. Samson did not need elaborate weaponry to defeat his enemies; he just used what was available at the time. Many Christians are afraid to take a stand because they feel outnumbered, but what they fail to realize is that God is the difference maker. Not only is the enemy outnumbered, but we can defeat him with whatever God has placed in our hands.

Stop thinking you have to have it all together to overcome your obstacles. Stop belittling yourself because you feel inadequate, considering your enemy's weapons superior to your own. Stop elevating the size of your enemy, and start elevating the size of your God. Start bullying the bully of fear in your life. Go kick that Devil's butt and take no prisoners. You cannot lose because you have already won.

This is God's intentions, as can be seen in the Book of Genesis: "And I will put enmity between you and the woman, and between your offspring and hers; he will crush your head and you will strike his heel" (Gen. 3:15 NIV). We are the ones who are supposed to do the crushing, not Satan.

If you have been allowing the spirit of fear to have its way in your life, I challenge you to rise up and go kick that Devil in his teeth. Go walk in the power of the Holy Spirit and trample on the kingdom of darkness, banging on hell's gate looking for a fight. That is what a bully does; he goes around picking on those who are weaker. Well, Satan only has the power we give him. We possess a power that is greater than this world has ever seen. Flex your spiritual muscles, open your mouth, and proclaim you are taking back your city for Christ, daring the Devil to cross the boundaries you set.

Some may say I am exaggerating, and that we could not possibly do what I am suggesting. God's Word says, "No, in all these things we are more than conquerors through him who loved us" (Rom. 8:37 NIV). The definition of the word conqueror is a person who conquers; a winner. This does not sound like someone who runs and hides in a corner, praying to God for some relief. No, this sounds like someone who knows who he is and what he is capable of. This sounds like a person who seeks a challenge. These are the people who go looking for a fight because they know in the end they win. We are instructed to "Therefore put on the full armor of God, so that when the day of evil comes, you may be able to stand your ground, and after you have done everything, to stand" (Eph. 6:13 NIV). Too many Christians are lying down in defeat when they need to be standing in holy boldness, staring down the enemy who dares to defy them. This is what David asked when he said, "Who is this uncircumcised Philistine, that he should defy the armies of the living God" (1 Sam. 17:26)? Each of us should be asking the spirit of fear, the spirit of low self-esteem, the spirit of debt and lack, and the spirit of sickness, "How dare you defy the son or daughter of the living God?"

Still not convinced? Let's take a look at another mighty man of God and his reaction to giants. Moses sent out twelve spies to survey the land God promised to give the children of Israel. When they returned, ten came back with a negative report, but Joshua and Caleb had a positive report. "And Caleb stilled the people before Moses, and he said, let us go up at once and possess it; for we are well able to overcome it" (Num. 13:30). Notice Caleb did not need time to think the situation over; neither did he have to pray, asking the Lord if it was His will if they should go in and take the land. No, he knew their time had come and they need not worry about their adversary because the Lord had already given them the victory. I find it interesting that Caleb said, "Let us go up at once." Fear will always hesitate, but faith takes action now. This is why the Bible says, "Now faith is" (Heb. 11:1). Faith acts in the present, looking to take hold of something in its future.

God's promises are like commercials that He broadcast in our spirits. When He does this, He is showing us the result of our faith. By faith, we must trust Him by walking in the steps He has ordained for us in order to see the dream materialize. Fear wants to stop our God-given dreams from ever coming to past, which is why we must take an aggressive stance and bully the bully of fear.

There is no such thing as a no win situation with God. He loves to perform the miraculous when it seems as if all the chips are against His people, primarily so He can get the glory. In the Book of Judges God told Gideon to reduce the amount of troops down to three hundred men. Scripture says, "And the Lord said unto Gideon, the people that are with thee are too many for me to give the Midianites into their hands, lest Israel vaunt themselves against me; saying, mine own hand hath saved me" (Jud. 7:2). God is going to get the glory out of your life. The question is, will you trust Him to help you defeat every enemy in your life, regardless of how bad the situation looks or how outnumbered you may be?

The days of allowing the spirit of fear to have its way in your life are over. The time to take action is now, not tomorrow. God has given us His Spirit and His Word; now we must walk in the authority that has been given to us. Shrinking back is not an option. Be bold. Be aggressive, and take no prisoners as you bully the bully that has wreaked havoc in your life for too long.

Personal Points

During the summer months in Tennessee, it is not difficult to encounter a swarm of flying gnats. These little insects are a nuisance, especially when you are trying to enjoy some rest and relaxation outside. When I was in college, my roommate gave me the nickname the human gnat because I was always in people's face trying to instigate things. This is the same attitude God wants us to have toward the Devil. Instead of running from a defeated Devil, God wants us to get to the point where we are all in Satan's face, making it difficult for him to accomplish what he seeks to carry out in the earth. We should get on his nerves so much that every time he sees us coming, he starts running the other way.

Fear's Greatest Enemy

As believers, we are called to exercise our faith, trusting God will cause us to be victorious in every situation. Faith is our lifeline: without it, we cannot be called believers. Knowing this, there is still one thing that can trump our faith, and it is fear's greatest enemy, which is love. The love of God is a shield to all who call upon Him. It is our peace, our refuge, and our strong tower. When we walk in love as we are instructed, every fear is expelled and loses its power. "There is no fear in love. But perfect love drives out fear, because fear has to do with punishment. The one who fears is not made perfect in love" (1 John 4:18 NIV). Several things stand out in this verse. First, it is worth mentioning there is no fear in love. When we receive God's love and allow that love to flow through us, the spirit of fear has no power over us. Most of the time when the spirit of fear speaks, it says things such as, "You're not going to make it," "How are you going to pay your bills?" or "It's over for you." We all know these are lies, but quite often, many of us believe them, which shows we have not fully accepted the fact that God loves us. If we know God loves us, we would not worry about how our bills are going to be paid or if we were going to make it. God promises to never leave us nor forsake us (Heb. 13:5). God is not a deadbeat dad; He takes care of His children. He knows our every need, and He wants us to rely on Him to meet those needs. King David was so true when he said, "I have never seen the righteous forsaken, or their children begging for bread" (Psalm 37:25 NIV). Think back for a moment when you were a child and you had been at school all day. Never did the thought cross your mind how you were going to eat. You knew your parents would provide for you. A person who walks in fear has yet to come to the understanding that God loves him and He will provide for him. Scripture says, "If you, then, though you are evil, know how to give good gifts to your children, how much more will your Father in heaven give good gifts to those who ask him" (Matt. 7:11 NIV). If you have allowed the spirit of fear to rattle you, causing you to doubt God's ability to care for you and meet your needs, I challenge you to take an inventory of all the times He has come through, and allow His peace to flood your soul.

Perfect love drives out fear. We may ask, "What is perfect love?" The only definition I can use comes from 1 Corinthians 13:4-8: "Love is patient, love is kind. It does not envy, it does not boast, it is not proud. It does not dishonor others, it is not self-seeking, it is not easily angered, it keeps no record of wrongs. Love does not delight in evil but rejoices with the truth. It always protects, always trusts, always hopes, always perseveres. Love never fails." When we begin to walk in love as instructed in God's Word, we will see every fear in our lives driven away. One of the reasons so many Christians walk in fear could be that we have a misunderstanding of love. Many have allowed the world to define what love is, but the world cannot give nor define what it does not have. Love comes from God and God is love, which is why fear cannot occupy the same space as God. The very meaning of the phrase "drive out" is to send, expel, or otherwise cause to move by force or compulsion. Fear is expelled from God's presence whenever He shows up. This can happen every time if we commit to walking in love.

1 John 4:18 says, "Fear has to do with punishment." Whenever we walk in fear, it is proof we have forgotten who we are in Christ. Scripture says, "There is therefore now no condemnation to them that are in Christ Jesus" (Rom. 8:1). The spirit of fear will always lie to us, making us think God is mad at us and we could not possibly be forgiven for our sins. This is far from the truth. Jesus died for our past, present, and future sins. He knew everything we would ever do before we were born, and yet He still gave His life for each of us. The spirit of fear hopes we are ignorant of what God has provided for us by way of the cross, and Satan will bombard our minds in an attempt to cause confusion in our lives. Sometimes Satan will even use Christians whose mind has not been renewed by the

Word of God to accuse us of things God has already forgiven us for. Regardless of the vessel the accusations come from, remind yourself that every sin is under the blood and God does not even remember them. God hurls all our iniquities into the depths of the sea (Micah 7:19 NIV). People who are led by the spirit of fear think they have to do something in order to atone for their mistakes, but God has already taken care of that. Allow this statement to sink into your spirit: "You are already forgiven; and there is nothing left to be done!"

God's record is flawless, and His name speaks for itself. He is merciful and gracious, longsuffering and abundant in goodness and truth (Exodus 34:6). The spirit of fear cannot compare to God, and once believers accept this fact, our lives will go to levels that are off the charts. God will never stop loving us, no matter what wrongs we may commit. God's love is greater than any sin we may commit and any lie the enemy will utter. Knowing this should bring comfort to our souls and give us a holy boldness. The spirit of fear cannot and will not have its way in our lives another day as we remind ourselves of God's love, and we walk in His love.

Personal Points

As mentioned in a previous chapter, I use to be gripped by the spirit of fear and would condemn myself for things God had already forgiven me for. The way I overcame this was by verbally speaking what God's Word said about me. Each of us must fill our hearts with God's Word, and speak His Word aloud. Something happens when we speak the Word of God aloud. Three individuals hear us whenever we do this: God, Satan, and ourselves. When we agree with God by accepting His Word as the truth, all of hell becomes nervous. Satan knows he is now dealing with someone who can inflict some serious damage to his kingdom, and he becomes afraid.

Take Action Now

In the world in which we live, it has become increasingly difficult to be a Christian. In the past, the persecution of Christians was something that happened in some far away foreign land, where the people did not serve nor know God. Now, within America, a country that was established on Christian principles, we have laws being passed that are anti-God. Laws that support abortion, same sex marriage, and those that seek to silence pastors or other Christians who condemn sinful acts. Our enemy has advanced within every level of government, from the Supreme Court, Congress, and even the White House. No longer can we rely on government to protect us. If the truth be told, government is working in conjunction with the adversary. The world's system is not for God; neither can it be, for Satan and those who serve him control it. Believers can no longer sit idly by, allowing wickedness to go unchecked. For far too long, many Christians have allowed a faithful few to fight on the front lines, but this must stop and it must stop now! If we desire our way of life to continue, we must take action to protect the liberties we currently have, and work to overturn laws that go against the will of God. Too many Christians have allowed the spirit of fear to push them around, and it has cost us our children, our schools, and our neighborhoods. Sadly, many followers of Christ have become lazy, expecting everything to be given to them. That is not how the kingdom of God operates. Even the children of Israel had to fight for the land God promised them. They could not sit back and expect God to hand everything over to them.

In order to preserve our way of life, it will take a new breed of Christian to stand in the face of adversity and say, "We may have allowed you to get away with things in the past, but those days are over." There may be times when we will suffer great losses, and some may lose their lives, but any loss we suffer on this side of glory will be richly rewarded on the other side. My question for you is, how much is God's kingdom worth to you? Sure, we all have obligations that must be met-obligations to our employers and our families, but our first obligation is to God. Just going to church is not enough. We come to church to be taught so that we might go out into the world to serve.

Jesus said, "The harvest is plentiful but the workers are few" (Matt. 9:37 NIV). We must be about our Father's business for the great day is fast approaching. By doing nothing, we are allowing the spirit of fear to succeed in what it was sent to accomplish – which is to silence Christians. We cannot drop the ball. Too much is at stake. A generation yet to be born is depending on us to stand up and reveal God to a dying world.

The Word of God says, "Defend the weak and the fatherless; uphold the cause of the poor and the oppressed. Rescue the weak and the needy; deliver them from the hand of the wicked" (Psalm

82:3-4 NIV). These instructions were given to believers, not sinners. All of hell laughs at us when we do not act on God's Word. Let's shut them up, starting today. I challenge everyone reading this book to step out and allow God to use you to change the world for His glory.

About the Author

Charles Roberts is a member of Faith is the Victory Church in Nashville Tennessee, where he proudly serves under the leadership of Pastor Charles Cowan. He is a graduate of Middle Tennessee State University and Cumberland University, where he received his Master of Science degree in Public Service Management. Charles' mission is simple: "To change the world for the glory of God," and he seeks to accomplish this through writing and public speaking. He is a strong advocate for families and longs to see Christians walk in everything that God's Word says belongs to us. For more information, visit his Website at *www.charlesrobertsonline.com*

You Don't Intimidate Me

Please send all correspondence to:

printersway@yahoo.com

Or

2817 West End Ave Ste 126-217

Nashville, TN 37203

Receive The Gift

If you have not made the decision to make Jesus the Lord of your life and you would like to do so, repeat this prayer now.

Heavenly Father, your Word says, *"If thou confess with thy mouth the Lord Jesus, and shalt believe in thine heart that God hath raised him from the dead, thou shalt be saved. For with the heart man believeth unto righteousness; and with the mouth confession is made unto salvation" (Rom. 10:9-10).* Lord, I do believe that Jesus died for my sins and I receive your gift of salvation. I make you the Lord of my life and I look forward to walking with you all the days of my life.

Thank You Lord!

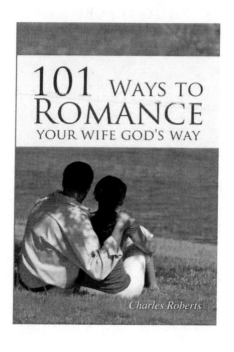

I wrote *101 Ways to Romance Your Wife God's Way* to encourage men to show greater appreciation in the gift of their wives that God has given to them. More often than not, most men stop courting or pursuing their wives after they are married. But Jesus never stops pursuing His bride, and neither should men stop pursuing their wives. After listening firsthand to countless women state their frustration about their husband's lack of passion, I saw the need to remind men that our job of showing affection for the one we love is a lifetime commission! Men, romancing your wife may have started during your courtship, but that was just the jump-start to a lifetime of romantic adventure. I want couples to fall in love again every day. Check out the very easy tips and suggestions contained within its pages.

Some of the tips include:

• Call your wife throughout the day. Let her know how much you miss her and how much you appreciate all that she does. #4

• Take her to the place where the two of you first met and reenact as much of the entire experience as you can remember. #44

• Make a point to hug her at least three times a day. #59

• Kiss her hand in public. #60

• Pray with her every night before you go to bed. #43

• Stop by your wife's job just to say hello. #25

Take Authority was written to encourage readers to walk in the authority Jesus died to give you. Christians are to be the spiritual authority figures in the earth, but in order for you to walk in that level of authority; we must first conquer certain things in the natural.

First, this book will challenge you to examine yourself and address natural issues such as time management, money management, and to make better decisions when it comes to your health. Once these basic and yet challenging things are under better control, God will have no problem giving us greater levels of victory over spiritual things.

Take Authority will equip you to be proactive in your walk with God and set you on the path to be everything God has called you to be.

Chapter Titles

The Authority of the Believer

Take Authority over Your Life

Take Authority over Your Home

Take Authority over Your Health

Take Authority over Your Time

Take Authority over Your Community

FAITH FORWARD

CHARLES ROBERTS

Faith Forward was written to encourage Christians to move forward with their God-given vision despite the obstacles they face. God is the Master Gardener, who consistently plants dreams within the hearts of His people. That's the good news for us. The reality is that there will always be an adversary to the promises of God. Knowing this, we only have one sound, justifiable choice, and that is to go forward in faith. Just like we cannot drive a car forward and in reverse at the same time, neither can we trust God and doubt Him at the same time.

This book will encourage you to ignore your critics while pursuing your promises. It will motivate you to keep going even when your circumstances are screaming for you to give up.

Faith Forward will also encourage you to believe in yourself even when no one else does.

Finally, *Faith Forward* will challenge you to keep your eyes on the reward and not the opposition that you face.

Chapter Titles

Have Faith In God

Believe In Yourself

Don't Stop!

Faith is a One-Way Street

Stand Trial

Big Giants Equal Big Prizes

Ignore Your Critics

Lighten Your Load

It Can Bloom Again

Be Not Ashamed But Don't Flaunt

EVERY MAN
IS NOT A HUSBAND

EVERY WOMAN
IS NOT A WIFE

CHARLES ROBERTS

I wrote *Every Man is Not a Husband - Every Woman is Not a Wife*, so that people might know what a true husband and wife should look like from a Biblical perspective and so they might look at marriage God's Way.

Our society today is flooded with images of what men and women should look for when choosing a spouse and how they should act once they are married.

• The world says that if we feel a connection, then we should follow our heart.

• The world says as long as a man provides, then he is a good catch.

• The world says that it is okay to sleep together before you are married.

The problem is anytime you take advice from the world; you end up with the world's results. God wants us to thrive, especially in our marriages. Marriage is a gift from God and it is not to be entered into lightly.

Countless television shows and movies have been created where men are depicted as either womanizers, or their actions are so immature, they are viewed no different than children.

Women are sometimes depicted as either hyper-controlling or promiscuous and carefree.

It is within marriage that:

- We walk in forgiveness daily.

- We are instructed to submit ourselves to one another.

- We are to walk in unconditional love.

All of these should draw us closer to God, which is why God values marriage, and which is why I believe this book is desperately needed now more than ever.

Chapter Titles

Let's Go Fishing

Good, Better, and Best

Sex and Deception

Tug of War

Marriage Misunderstood

What Women Want

What Men Want